What Is a Heat Wave?

Robin Johnson

Crabtree Publishing Company
www.crabtreebooks.com

Author: Robin Johnson

Publishing plan research and development: Reagan Miller

Editors: Reagan Miller and Kathy Middleton

Proofreaders: Janine Deschenes

Design and photo research: Samara Parent

Prepress technician: Samara Parent

Print and production coordinator: Kathy Berti

Photographs
iStock: p6; p20; p21; p22
Shutterstock: p12 © De Visu

All other images from Shutterstock

About the author
Robin Johnson has written more than 60 educational books for children. She plans to keep writing books and chasing rainbows— whatever the weather.

Library and Archives Canada Cataloguing in Publication

Johnson, Robin (Robin R.), author
    What is a heat wave? / Robin Johnson.

(Severe weather close-up)
Includes index.
Issued in print and electronic formats.
ISBN 978-0-7787-2397-4 (bound).--ISBN 978-0-7787-2435-3
(paperback).--ISBN 978-1-4271-1750-2 (html)

    1. Heat waves (Meteorology)--Juvenile literature. I. Title.

QC981.8 A5 J65 2016   j551.5'253   C2015-908678-7
                                             C2015-908679-5

Library of Congress Cataloging-in-Publication Data

CIP available at the Library of Congress

Crabtree Publishing Company

Printed in Canada/032016/EF20160210

www.crabtreebooks.com   1-800-387-7650

Published in Canada
Crabtree Publishing
616 Welland Ave.
St. Catharines, Ontario
L2M 5V6

Published in the United States
Crabtree Publishing
PMB 59051
350 Fifth Avenue, 59th Floor
New York, New York 10118

Published in the United Kingdom
Crabtree Publishing
Maritime House
Basin Road North, Hove
BN41 1WR

Published in Australia
Crabtree Publishing
3 Charles Street
Coburg North
VIC 3058

Contents

Golden Sun

What would we do without the Sun? It wakes us up in the morning. It brightens our days. The Sun helps our gardens grow. It makes us feel happy—except when it **melts** our snowmen and ice-cream cones!

Heat and light

The Sun warms Earth and everything on it. It gives us heat and light. Light from the Sun is called sunlight. Without sunlight, Earth would be cold and dark. No people, animals, or plants could survive.

Everyone loves the Sun!

5

What is weather?

Sunlight is part of the **weather**. Weather is what the air and sky are like in a certain place at a certain time. Clouds, rain, **wind**, and **temperature** are other parts of weather. Wind is moving air. Temperature is a measure of how hot or cold something is.

Hot and cold

The amount of sunlight in an area affects the temperature. When there is a lot of sunlight, the temperature is high. High temperatures make the air outside feel hot. When there is little sunlight, the temperature is low. Low temperatures make the air outside feel cold.

We use **thermometers** to measure temperature in units called **degrees**. The red bar moves up when the temperature gets warmer and down when the temperature gets colder.

What do you Think?

Which of these thermometers would you see on a hot, sunny day?

The atmosphere

All parts of weather take place in the **atmosphere**. The atmosphere is a large band of air that surrounds Earth. This band of air is always pushing down on the planet. This pushing force is called **air pressure**. Air pressure is different in different places.

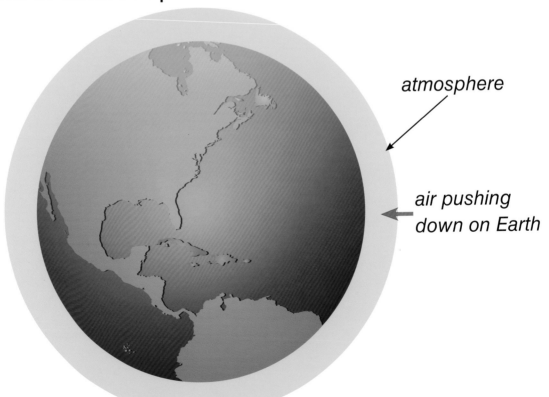

atmosphere

air pushing down on Earth

Under pressure

When air pressure changes, it brings different weather. Low air pressure brings rainy or snowy weather. High air pressure brings sunshine and nice weather. When a place has high air pressure for a long time, a lot of hot air is trapped near the ground. This trapped air can cause a **heat wave**.

*We use tools called **barometers** to measure air pressure.*

CAUTION!
EXTREME
HEAT
DANGER

What is a heat wave?

A heat wave is a long period of very hot weather. It can last for several days or for weeks. During a heat wave, the temperature in an area is higher than normal. **Humidity** is often high. Humidity is the amount of **water vapor** in the air. High humidity makes the air feel sticky and the temperature feel even higher than the reading on the thermometer.

Severe weather

A heat wave is a type of **severe weather**. Severe weather is dangerous weather that can harm people and animals. It can cause damage to buildings and land. Learning what to do if there is a heat wave where you live is the best way to stay safe.

Severe heat bakes the ground. It can even crack roads!

Summer heat

In big cities, buildings and roads **absorb**, or soak up, heat during the day. At night, the heat rises into the air, keeping the temperature high when it would normally be cooling down.

Heat waves happen during the summer. There are more hours of sunlight in summer than in any other **season**. More sunlight means higher temperatures during the day. Nights are shorter in summer, so there is less time for the weather to cool down after the Sun sets.

Around the world

Heat waves happen in many parts of the world, including the United States and Canada. These places have hot summers—but heat waves make them even hotter! In some parts of the world, long periods of high temperatures are part of the usual weather. A heat wave in one part of the world may be just normal weather in areas with hot climates.

The Philippines has a hot climate. It has only 2 seasons: a rainy season, and a dry one.

13

Droughts

There is usually no rain or other **precipitation** during a heat wave. Precipitation is water that falls from the clouds. If a heat wave lasts a long time, it can cause a **drought**. A drought is a long period of time without rain.

*A **wildfire** is a large fire that spreads quickly. During a heat wave, the flames spread quickly because dry land catches fire and burns easily.*

On dry land

During droughts, green grass and leaves turn brown. Crops dry up and die. Crops are plants grown by farmers for food. When crops die, there is less food to eat in that area. If there is no rain for a very long time, rivers and lakes dry up.

When water sources dry up, there is less water than people and animals need to live.

What do you Think?

Why is it important to use less water during a drought?

Heat dangers

Heat waves are dangerous for people and animals. You can get sunburns, rashes, or cramps from the Sun and heat. You can get **dehydrated**. That means your body does not have enough water to work as it should. You can also get a serious illness called **heat stroke**. Heat stroke happens when the temperature of your body gets too high.

Heat waves are dangerous for animals, too! Bring your pets inside or make sure they have shady spots to rest outside. Give them plenty of cool water to drink.

No sweat

Your body must stay cool to work properly. You sweat to cool your body's temperature. Sweat is water that **evaporates**, or changes to water vapor in the air. When the humidity is high, the sweat cannot evaporate easily. There is already too much moisture in the air. The sweat stays on your skin and makes it harder for you to cool down.

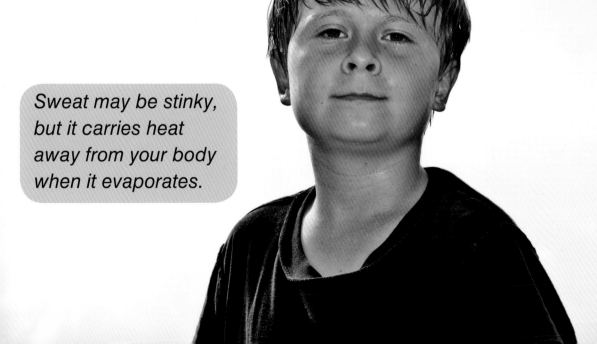

Sweat may be stinky, but it carries heat away from your body when it evaporates.

Keep your cool

It is important to keep cool during heat waves. Drink plenty of water, even if you do not feel thirsty. Try to stay indoors in buildings that have air conditioning. Take cold baths or showers to cool down. Avoid going outdoors or playing sports during heat waves.

Libraries, movie theaters, shopping malls, and other public places usually have air conditioning. You can go to these cool places to beat the heat.

Beat the heat

If you must go outside, stay out of the hot Sun. Put on sunscreen so your skin does not burn. Wear a hat to protect your head from the Sun. Avoid wearing dark colors because they absorb the Sun's rays and heat you up. Rest under trees and other places that give you shade.

If you must go outside during a heat wave, carry an umbrella for shade.

19

Studying weather

Meteorologists warn people when heat waves will happen in their area. Meteorologists are scientists who study weather. They use thermometers and other tools to measure and **predict** weather. They share the weather reports on television, on the radio, and online.

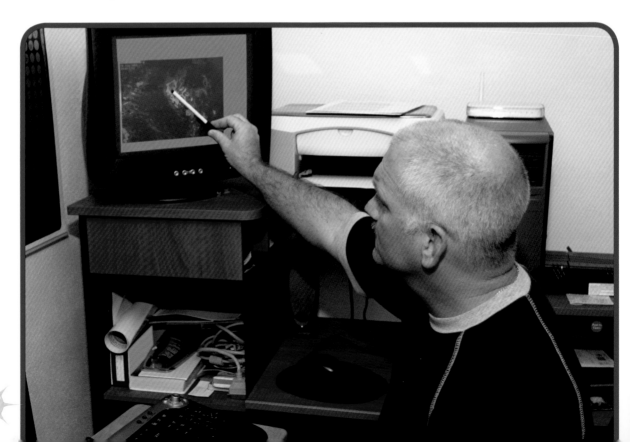

Cooler in the shade

Meteorologists tell people to rest in shaded areas when they are outdoors in hot weather. Why is it important to stay in the shade? Do you think the temperature is higher in the Sun or in the shade? Do the experiment on the next page to find out!

THE WORLD NEWS

Since 1883   YOUR NUMBER ONE SOURCE FOR HEADLINES $1.00

HEAT WAVE

FORECASTERS PREDICT RECORD TEMPERATURES

LOCAL AUTHORITIES ON ALERT FOR HEAT RELATED CONCERNS

CITIZENS URGED TO STAY INSIDE AND DRINK PLENTY OF WATER

Cool experiment!

Get two ice cubes that are the same size and shape. Put each ice cube in a separate dish and take the dishes outside. Set one dish in the shade and the other in the sunlight. Watch both ice cubes carefully. They will melt when the temperature gets high enough. Which ice cube melts faster? What does that tell you about the temperature in sunlight and shade?

What do you Think?

Why would an ice cube melt faster in a black dish than a white one? (Turn to page 19 for a clue.)

Learning more

Books

Drought and Heat Wave Alert by Paul Challen. Crabtree Publishing Company, 2004.

Hammered by a Heat Wave by Laura DeLallo. Bearport Publishing, 2010.

What is temperature? by Robin Johnson. Crabtree Publishing Company, 2013.

Websites

This useful fact sheet tells you what to do before, during, and after a heat wave: **www.ready.gov/kids/know-the-facts/extreme-heat**

Be a weather whiz kid and learn about temperature, heat waves, and more: **www.weatherwizkids.com/weather-temperature.htm**

Learn how to beat the heat and stay safe in the Sun at: **http://kidshealth.org/kid/watch/out/summer_safety.html#**

Play this fun Dr. Seuss game to learn about the Sun, temperature, and other parts of weather: **http://pbskids.org/catinthehat/games/weather-transformer.html**

Words to know

Note: Some boldfaced words are defined where they appear in the book.

barometer (buh-ROM-i-ter) noun A tool used to measure air pressure

climate (KLAHY-mit) noun The weather that an area has had for a long period of time

degrees (dih-GREES) noun Units of measurement that are marked on a measuring tool, such as a thermometer or barometer

heat wave (HEET weyv) noun A period of unusually high temperatures and humidity

melt (melt) verb To change from solid to liquid form by heating

predict (pri-DIKT) verb To tell what will happen before it takes place

season (SEE-zuhn) noun A time of year with certain weather and temperatures

thermometer (ther-MOM-i-ter) noun A tool used to measure temperature

water vapor (WAW-ter VEY-per) noun A thin mist of water in the air

A noun is a person, place, or thing. A verb is an action word that tells you what someone or something does. An adjective is a word that tells you what something is like.

Index

31901059271546